WHISPERS OF THE HEART

DR NILANJAN ROY

To the hearts that yearn and the souls that ache,

To those who embrace love's tender quake,

This collection of whispers, a testament to tears,

Is for you, whose stories dance through the years.

In every verse, may you find your own grace,

In each line, a mirror of your embrace.

For it is in our shared pain and delight,

That we discover the essence of love's light.

Contents

Foreword

In the delicate tapestry of life, where threads of joy and sorrow intertwine, **"Whispers of the Heart"** emerges as a profound reflection on the human experience. This collection invites readers into a realm where love's ebbs and flows are captured with both raw honesty and tender grace.

Nilanjan Roy, a family physician whose life has been marked by both professional dedication and personal metamorphosis, channels his journey into these poignant verses. Each poem is a testament to the deep well of emotions that define our most intimate moments—moments of longing, connection, and transformation.

As you delve into these pages, you will encounter the echoes of heartfelt whispers that resonate with the universal truths of love and vulnerability. Roy's words invite you to explore the beauty of the human heart, to reflect on the dance between joy and melancholy, and to find solace in the shared experience of love's complexities.

May this collection offer you both comfort and inspiration, as it has for those who have had the privilege of reading it. **For an alternative experience, you might consider reading the poems in reverse order.** Start from the last poem and read all the way to the beginning, explore how the emotions evolve and intertwine in a new sequence.

Welcome to **"Whispers of the Heart,"** where every whisper tells a story of love and longing.

Preface

"Whispers of the Heart" is born from the intersection of my dual worlds as a family physician and a poet. My journey through the realms of healing and human connection has profoundly shaped my understanding of love, longing, and the myriad emotions that colour our lives. This collection is a reflection of my evolution—marked by moments of joy, sorrow, and profound insight.

In these pages, you will find a tapestry of emotions woven from the experiences that have moulded me. Each poem is a testament to the delicate balance between the elation of love and the depth of its challenges. Through vivid imagery and heartfelt reflections, I have sought to capture the essence of our shared human experience—moments of connection and disconnection, hope and despair.

As you read, I invite you to journey with me through the whispers of love that have echoed in my heart. May these verses offer you solace, inspiration, and a deeper understanding of the beauty and complexity of our emotional lives. This collection is both a personal exploration and an open invitation to find resonance in the echoes of your own heart.

Thank you for joining me in this intimate exploration.

Acknowledgements

Writing "**Whispers of the Heart**" has been a journey of introspection and expression, and I am deeply grateful to those who have been a part of this endeavour.

To my family and friends, your unwavering support and encouragement have been my anchor. Your belief in my work has given me the courage to explore the depths of my emotions and share them with the world.

To my mentors and colleagues in both medicine and literature, your wisdom and insights have been invaluable. You have inspired me to blend my professional experiences with my passion for poetry, creating a collection that is both heartfelt and profound.

And to my readers, thank you for opening your hearts to these poems. Your connection to my words makes this journey worthwhile.

This book is a reflection of many voices, and I am profoundly thankful for each one.

Prologue

In the quiet moments between dusk and dawn, where dreams intermingle with reality, love finds its voice. "**Whispers of the Heart**" is born from this ethereal space—a collection that delves into the silent symphonies of the soul. These poems explore the delicate balance of joy and sorrow, the tender embrace of passion, and the bittersweet echoes of longing.

Each verse is a fragment of my journey, shaped by the highs and lows of life, love, and self-discovery. As you turn these pages, may you find a reflection of your own heart's whispers, and may the words within offer solace, understanding, and a touch of timeless beauty.

1. Unspoken Feelings

Mesmerizing eyes, unaware thoughts,
Forgotten promises, crocodile tears,
Tearing the grip apart, lost in emotions,
Lost the peace, love is the only thing that lies.
Unspoken actions, louder cries,
Falls apart the beautiful mind.
Hating was new, hatred the only truth,
Love was to be shown, cared to be anew.
Conversations were old, communication still anew,
Not to be a part, but to apart.
Distractions were many, choices were on you,
Carried by the flow, cared for someone new.
Love is the only thing that hides the truth,
Blinded by the dazzle, glared by the reflection,
Left the heart with no emotions.
Mind being late to know, body falls apart before it comes true.
Love was the only truth, fights to keep but fails to fight for you.
Choices were made, I was among the few,
Will let you go, to the love that was always anew.

2. Destined Bonds

Lovers being new, love being old,
Smashed my dreams into peace,
But still can't stop loving you.
With broken pieces of heart.
Never wanna go back, never wanna hug you,
But I, the only one, care for you.
Never fear of losing me, I'll always stay,
Never come back, love has changed its way.
Let me love you... let me look at you
I like the way you look at me,
I love the way you wear my favourite gifts,
But stories crafted never speak the truth.
Lovers being new, love being old,
Move on with your love, I'll always be there for you.
Love is all I did, love is what I care,
I don't wanna lose you, I don't wanna have you back.
Misunderstanding being the leash,
Guides through the darkness, to fade its glow,
love this world, till it loves back to you.
Lovers can sacrifice, love will always be anew.
Destinations were different but destined to you,
Memories were same, friends being chaotic,

Love being shared, still it holds on to you

3. Longing for you

Baby, it all started with calls with unspoken feelings,
Under the tree by the side of the hostel gate, waiting for you.
I wish I never called you, wish I could skip getting scars,
With a mind that scalped a wound. Baby, it hurts, loving hurts.
If you love me, wait for me. Until then, keep the memories fresh,
With the ebb and flow till the moment we connect anew.
Memories that were vivid in mind, letting them fade is still new
for me.
Let me run through the veins back into the heart,
Till the moment I find you there, cozy with you.
Live a life that we will always remember.
Don't let me down with insecurities and doubts of lies.
The memories that were still fresh take time to fade.
Don't let me go, don't make me unlove the person I owe,
Lone in an empty heart filled with emotions, to make it a part.
Hides in the laughter, of the face, that was a liar.
Give me a night to be alone, keep the thoughts with you,
Pricking my heart with pain I could always remember.
Don't hide the face, don't take the love, wake me from the
dream,
That it fades, hope it's not true, a reel that will never be true.
Underneath the hat was the woman I fell into,

Thought to be happier and happier with you.

4. Transformation

Face coloured, gloomy inside,
Take a deep breath, let the smoke glide.
Let her go, he cried, with pain that resides,
The hurdle within, is the unease that won't hide.
From darkness to daylight, wake me up
Through the journey of life,
Through and through, you created anew,
Stoned my heart that hardly feels for you.

.

5. Pure Love

My life is beautiful, my love is pure,
I saw an angel—I saw you.
Your smile, so beautiful,
Fades the pain that leaves the happiness with you.
Take care, my princess, take care of my love,
It's pure, it's virgin, it's new—it's you, love.
Take a deep breath and let it go,
With the world aside, just you and me.
Abid in the muse, it still feels new

6. Cherishing Love

I still remember the day we kissed
under the sky full of stars,
on the terrace to hug u back,
Beauty of nature being faded in front of u,
i love you, i still love you,
missing that moments spends with you.
The ride on bike being the memories,
nature being celebrating our intimacies,
the way being too long,
nature being too amorous brings the rain out of emotion.
Cant sleep in night cant forget your eyes,
love is the only thing i like,
darkness of your eyes is the depth of love,
attire being new, friends being waiting,
cake still like anew,
intimacies r still virgin like a few.
Tears being rolling down, emotions being outraged,
I the only one to feel the same,
love being common, destinations being different,
story being crafted can never be the same...

7. Romantic Love

In the moonlight, where shadows play,
I see your face, every single day.
My heart beats fast, my soul feels alive,
In your eyes, my heart finds a home to thrive

8. Echoes of love

Intimacies shared by the clouds embark
On outraged love, flowing tears through the rain.
Let's embrace the intimacies, for love is meant to be shared,
Beneath the celestial canvas.
Holding your hands to bring you closer,
To kiss you on your lips,
Intimacies witnessed by the clouds,
Entwine the clouds with the moon's silvery glow,
To spread the shadows to the love that we make.

9. Lies

I love you...
I love you more than you, better than you,
Bending over, kissing you,
Getting high, fucking back on you.
I trust you, I need you, I care for you,
Let me lean on you, let me love you.
Don't flutter, never utter,
Hating you still matters.
You being my muse, you being my fiancé,
Love being my emotion, you being my distraction,
Can't love you deeply, can't sync with time,
Love being the only thing I lie.
I begged you, the love, the life,
portrait laid by speaks of life,
captures your hidden eyes
never spoke of truth but the lies.
Takes me back in time
to the memories till it gets fragile
hug me like a silent vibe....

10. Euphoric Love

Never smoke me too high to go down,
Never love so much to leave me apart,
Love me like a mysterious guy,
Waking up on a day to get high.
The euphoric nature of me takes you higher,
To another world, no one to choose,
No one to care about, only you and me,
Love and euphoria.
Never smoke too high to go down…
It's me, the weed, to care for you,
It's me, the rolling paper to make you high,
It's me, the weed to take you to a higher state of mind.
Love me or hate me, I will love you.
Nature being against me, I am with you.
It's me, marijuana.
Smoke me too high, never let me down….

11. Love's Beauty

Little did I know about you, smiling at me,
Looking back at you, I know I love you.
I want you, I need you, but somebody else is waiting for you.
The darkness of your eyes is the depth of love.
Deeper than the deepest ocean,
Mirrors a smile on the face
a gift of yours that will never fade

12. A long time

It's been a long time, we being together,
Holding hands, going high in the night,
And your immense love takes me back in time,
Having conversations over a glass of wine.
The darkness under the loom is the curse of you,
Fragrance beyond regret.
Can't see the face, can't touch the beauty,
You against all eternity, love beyond my ability.
The riot all around syncs with the fumes of cremation,
The beauty that fades cursed,
to be a part of me, to kill the sync with you.
It's been a long time since the sky shaded its tears,
With the darkest hue, man on fire, buses in the sky,
blasts being noisy, nature being the coolest.
Takes all the crimes, washed with tears,
No fear, only tears, going against you,
The riot which I can't bear.
It's been a long time, you take me high,
All above the sky, to make it like anew,
Broken apart, still a part,
I regret the scenes to be a nightmare like you.
The darkest hue can touch the dream,

But not me, to sync with you.
It's been a long time.

13. With You

Let me take your smile with me,
Let me paint your beauty till eternity,
Let me love the gloominess inside,
Let me dive deep to break that cage.
Let me make you fly to the end of the sky,
Let us escape this chaotic world,
Let us not fear the boundaries,
Let this world write a new story,
A story that can never fade.

14. Forever Love

Lost dreams can ever be pursued,
Your presence can never be anew,
It took me time to rise above the fantasy,
Dream being my passion, memories my enemy,
Everything you see is just anew,
Old memories are messed up like you.
It took me time to know the darkness beyond you,
My inabilities to make anew,
Hatred being the common, love being the difference,
You and me, abyss being portrayed,
of scars by the time I wrote it for you .
Love being taught, lovers being few,
Can dream a life to be anew.
Emotions being outraged, mind depressed,
My attire is only new.

15. Embracing the Paradox

*Never let someone get so close
that they overshadow your emotions and feelings
as time flows in a relationship.
The bonds once shared,
the emotions once invested,
are not truly what they deserve;
it's your expectations that hurt.
Envy the miseries
when bonds grow weak,
leashes that bleed when loosened,
sharp like a scalped wound,
scarring your feelings,
yet you hold it back.
Scared to lose it,
scared to love again,
drained and drenched with trauma
and unhealed scars that haunt.
Let time heal you.
Let your scars bleed for the one
who loves you more than you think you deserve.*

Feel the love, feel the emotions,
pamper yourself like never before.
Break the monotony
and embrace the happiness
you truly deserve.

16. Unexpressed Feelings

Dear,

Do you imagine how it will be?

longing a quest to feel free,

The highs and the lows, the love we vow,

Dreams once imagined, are truly what we owe.

Rare and precious, let's be slow

Thoughts once unspoken, are now true,

In love that brings peace, binds me and you.

Emotions once hidden now run through our veins,

Words unsaid yet louder than loud refrains.

In tones just for us, that no one else could hear,

Feelings once shared, now crystal and clear.

Caring once lost, partners felt blue,

But love, always cherished, begins anew.

Stay with me, stay by my side,

In feelings that linger where truth does reside.

You are my muse, my guiding flame,

Destinies entwined in love's sweet name.

Come closer, hold my hand,

Let us marry,

Witnessed by the fire which once let us apart,

In life's endless cycle, a bond from the heart.

A Heartfelt Gratitude

Thank you for joining me on this journey through "Whispers of the Heart." Your presence has been a source of strength and inspiration, and your engagement with these poems brings them to life in ways words alone cannot express.

In every line, every verse, I hope you find reflections of our shared emotions and experiences. Your support is a testament to the power of love and connection that these poems seek to celebrate.

May these words resonate with you as deeply as they have with me, and may we all continue to find beauty in the love that binds us.

With heartfelt gratitude,

Dr. Nilanjan Roy.

Closure

"In the silence of what's left unsaid,
I leave you with the love that's faded instead.
The whispers of what could've been true,
Are the softest goodbyes, I can give to you.
May the echoes of these pages carry our dreams,
Through the quiet spaces where love still gleams.
In every line, find a fragment of our shared grace,
A tender reminder of a love we embraced."

Poetically_loved By Saturn's_call

In the realm of ***Poetically_Loved***, where words dance on the wings of emotions, you'll find a haven crafted by ***Saturn's_Call***. Each poem is a constellation of feelings, inviting you to explore love's tender embrace, the ache of longing, and the beauty of life's fleeting moments. Follow the path of verses to discover more heartfelt whispers and let your soul be touched by the magic of poetry. Scan the QR code and step into a world where every line is a journey, and every word, is a cherished memory.

POETICALLY_LOVED

Follow for more content ❤?